THE LITTLE GUIDE TO

# HARRY STYLES

Published in 2024 by OH!
An Imprint of Welbeck Non-Fiction Limited,
part of Welbeck Publishing Group.
Offices in: London – 20 Mortimer Street, London W1T 3JW
and Sydney – Level 17, 207 Kent St, Sydney NSW 2000 Australia
www.welbeckpublishing.com

ISBN 978-1-80069-619-8

Compiled and written by: Malcolm Croft
Editorial: Victoria Denne
Project manager: Russell Porter
Production: Arlene Lestrade

A CIP catalogue record for this book is available from the British Library

Printed in China

10 9 8 7 6 5 4 3 2 1

THE LITTLE GUIDE TO

# HARRY STYLES

THE NEW KING OF POP

# CONTENTS

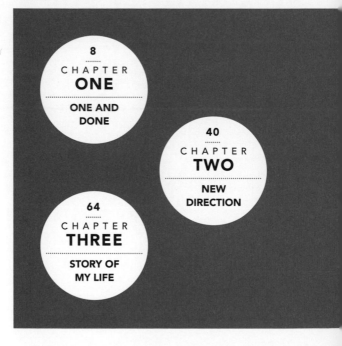

# INTRODUCTION

Harry Styles is the biggest superstar on the planet right now. To try to argue otherwise would be just silly, so don't bother.

After a couple of horrible years following the pandemic and an array of haunting global news events too miserable to highlight here, Harry stepped up and became the first real heart-robbin' hearthrob of the post-COVID world, the hero we all deserve right now, and one who could consistently cheer us all up with his cheeky charm and a handsome-ness that keeps most of his fans, young and old, up all night. And, judging by the deafening applause and acclaim he received after the release of his third solo album, the award-winning, multi-million-selling *Harry's House*, Mr Styles has brought with him enough X-factor to keep an entire generation of eyes gazing at his navel (despite, ironically, not having enough to win a TV show called *The X Factor* in 2010). Thankfully, Harry's a lovely young man too, worthy of all the fuss thrown at him, as this compact compendium will prove beyond all doubt.

This *Little Guide to Harry Styles* is a tiny tome so powerful it has squeezed the world's biggest star down to a snackable size, a perfect pick-me-up you can fondle in your hands whenever your Harry-shaped hole needs filling up or filling in. The book celebrates this 21st-century icon and inspiration in the only way we know how – in his own words, with more candid, compassionate and charm-filled quotes than you can shake one of his sequinned jumpsuits at, from his earliest interviews with One Direction… right through to what he said yesterday. Every part of his life-less-ordinary has been left undressed for your reading pleasure.

With a career-defining album and that almighty, world-beating Love On Tour jaunt completed in 2023 – and with Harry set to turn 30 in 2024 – whatever our boy does next will have the ears and eyes of the world. So, let's take a moment to remember him now – as *he* was – before the next amazing story of his life begins. Enjoy!

CHAPTER
**ONE**

# ONE AND DONE

In 2010, Harry Styles was a courageous 16-year-old standing in front of three (often cruel) musical gurus, and a televised audience of millions, asking to be judged on the spot for his singing ability and looks. Now, more than a decade later, that moment is enshrined in pop history as the arrival of a talent truly bubbling with that special sauce we call "X-factor".

Take a trip now down memory lane, and let the quotes unveiled in this chapter reintroduce the world's biggest boyband, One Direction, and, of course, its most famous face...

> **"**
>
> I was watching the year before, and I remember looking at the young guys on there – and I was kind of like, 'I'd love to have a go at it just to see what happens,' and that was kind of it. My mum actually did the application. And then three weeks later, I walked upstairs and she said, 'Oh, you've got your *X Factor* audition Sunday.' I was like, 'OK.'
>
> **"**

Harry, on learning of his *X Factor* audition, interview with Brian Hiatt, *Rolling Stone*, April 11, 2012.

66

I'm Harry Styles. I'm sixteen and I'm from Holmes Chapel in Cheshire.

99

Harry, his first ever words on TV, *X Factor* audition, April 11, 2010.

It was Harry's idea to call his former boyband One Direction.

"I thought it sounded good," Harry revealed on the CBS *Sunday Morning* show with host Tony Dokoupil in 2017.
"We threw around names for a little bit. I suggested One Direction, and everyone was like, 'Yeah we like that,' and then it kind of stuck, and that was it."

---

**"**

I went to the audition
to find out if I could
sing… or if my mum was
just being nice to me.

**"**

Harry, on his first *X Factor* audition, interview with Hamish
Bowles, *Vogue*, November 13, 2020.

---

66

In that instant, you're in the whirlwind. You don't really know what's happening; you're just a kid on the show. You don't even know you're good at anything. I'd gone because my mum told me I was good from singing in the car... but your mum tells you things to make you feel good, so you take it with a pinch of salt. I didn't really know what I was expecting when I went on there.

99

Harry, on his debut *X Factor* audition, interview with Cameron Crowe, *Rolling Stone*, April 18, 2017.

**"**

The craziest part about the whole *X Factor* fame is that it's so instant. The day before, you've never been on telly. Then suddenly you're a piece of national property. You don't think at the time, 'I should keep my personal stuff back for myself.' Partly because, if you're a 16-year-old who does that, you look like a jumped-up little shit. Can you imagine? 'Sorry, actually, I'd rather not comment…'

**"**

Harry, on overnight fame as a teenager, interview with Tom Lamont, *The Guardian*, December 14, 2019.

66

I was a kid, all I knew was I didn't have to go to school any more. I thought it was fucking great.

99

Harry, on becoming a member of 1D after *X Factor*, interview with Tom Lamont, *The Guardian*, December 14, 2019.

> **"**
> We were fuelling a machine.
> Keeping the fire going. When
> the band stopped, I realised
> that the thing I'd been missing,
> because it was all so fast-paced,
> was human connection.
> **"**

Harry, on the downsides of being in 1D, interview with
Tom Lamont, *The Guardian*, December 14, 2019.

After the release of
*Four* in 2014,
One Direction became
the first band in the
history of the
US *Billboard* charts
to have their first four
albums debut at No.1.

66

We all sat and watched the film of the Beatles arriving in America. And, to be honest, that really was like us. Stepping off the plane, the girls, the madness. It was exactly the same as when we got there – just 50 years earlier. Fame-wise, it's probably even bigger, but we don't stand anywhere near them in terms of music. We'd be total fools if we did.

99

Harry, on 1D's Beatle-esque mania, *Top of the Pops Magazine*, 2013.

66

We don't really do that.
We feel that objectifies
women and that's not
really what we're about.

99

Harry, when asked by a radio DJ if One Direction
calls "dibs" on girls, June 26, 2012.

**66**

We played the first Wembley show, and I remember I came off, got in the car, and just started crying because I was so disappointed. I was miserable.

**99**

Harry, on having tonsilitis during first 2013 Wembley performance with 1D, interview with Brittany Spanos, *Rolling Stone*, August 22, 2022.

**"**

I was 16 when One Direction started. I just finished school and didn't really know what it was that was happening. Everything was new and exciting and I didn't know how long everything was going to last. It was like, 'How long can we keep this going?' because I really didn't expect any of it to keep on happening.

**"**

Harry, on his career longevity, interview with Lynette Nylander, *Dazed and Confused*, November 15, 2021.

66

When I was in the band, I would have been afraid for everything to have stopped. I didn't necessarily know who I was if I wasn't in the band. Now, the idea of people telling me, 'We don't like your music anymore, go away,' doesn't scare me. I'm no longer working from a place of fear. I'm working from a place of wanting to try different things.

99

Harry, on being free from fear creatively, interview with Lynette Nylander, *Dazed and Confused*, November 15, 2021.

**"**

For a long time, I was scared of saying or doing the wrong thing, and how much trouble that would get me in. I was still growing up, making mistakes. I'm not ashamed of those things anymore. I've seen subconscious changes in a lot of places in my life.

**"**

Harry, on his time in 1D, interview with Lynette Nylander, *Dazed and Confused*, November 15, 2021.

---

**❝**

You are never on stage thinking, 'Yeah, this stadium's full because of me.'

**❞**

Harry, on being in a boyband, interview with Zane Lowe, Apple Music, May 17, 2022.

---

66

I look at artists who went through some version of what One Direction went through but on their own. I can't imagine having done that. I feel really lucky that we always had each other, this unit that felt like you could keep each other in check and you could just have someone else who gets it.

99

Harry, on being in a band, interview with Zane Lowe, Apple Music, May 17, 2022.

**"**

We're lucky that we do get on.
The relationship that I've grown with
these four boys who I didn't know
three years ago is absolutely insane.
I am very lucky that I get to spend
so much time with them. There
could have been one person who
just didn't get on with anyone and
no one liked, but it isn't like that.

**"**

Harry, on his 1D bandmates, Australia's *60 Minutes*,
June 29, 2014.

**"**

The fact that we've all achieved different things outside of the band says a lot about how hard we worked in it.

**"**

Harry, on his bandmates post 1D split, interview with Shirley Halperin, *Variety*, November 10, 2020.

> **“**
> Life in 1D had become like a
> Wes Anderson movie. Cut. Cut.
> New location. Quick cut.
> New location. Cut. Cut. Show.
> Shower. Hard cut. Sleep.
> **”**

Harry, on being in 1D at the end, interview with
Cameron Crowe, *Rolling Stone*, April 18, 2017.

**"**

This album has made me realize the Harry in 1D was kind of the digitized Harry, almost like a character.

**"**

Harry, on his debut album, interview with Cameron Crowe, *Rolling Stone*, April 18, 2017.

66

You're never going to get used
to walking into a room and
have people screaming at you.
There are a lot of things that
come with the life you could
get lost in. But you have to let
it be what it is. I've learnt not to
take everything too seriously.

99

Harry, on suddenly having screaming fans, interview with
Ella Alexander, *Vogue*, November 1, 2012.

> **"**
> I'm 100 percent in this band.
> I still want to be touring with
> One Direction in ten years.
> I'll be doing it until I'm old
> and people are telling me
> to stop.
> **"**

Harry, on 1D, Australia's *60 Minutes*, June 29, 2014.

66

You get moments all the time that kind of make you pinch yourself, some of them make you quite emotional.

99

Harry, on recording 1D's debut album *Up All Night*, interview with Tom Bryant, *Daily Mirror*, November 12, 2012.

66

When you look from the outside, especially if you're a skeptic of groups made through TV shows, which is fair enough, people don't see what we do on a daily basis, people don't see that we work seven days a week. I think from the outside, it looks so glamorous. But it's hard work.

Harry, on the pressures of being in a boyband, interview with Brian Hiatt, *Rolling Stone*, April 11, 2012.

**66**

We all know that we all have our roles, and we all know that without one of us, it wouldn't work.

**99**

Harry, on being in 1D, interview with Brian Hiatt, *Rolling Stone*, April 11, 2012.

**"**

I was the same guy before this. I was the same guy during and I'll be the same guy afterwards.

**"**

Harry, on fame, *One Direction: This Is Us*, 2013.

66

I would never say we'll never do anything again. Maybe at some point everyone will want to do something again, but it's better if it happens naturally. I would never rule that out. It's the most important, greatest thing that's ever happened to me, being in that band. It completely changed my life.

99

Harry, on a possible 1D reunion, interview with Paul McCartney, *Another Man*, June 7, 2017.

Harry's first ever *X Factor* audition in 2010 was Stevie Wonder's 'Isn't She Lovely'.

"With a bit of vocal coaching, I think you could be very good,"
said judge Simon Cowell afterwards.

Bit of an understatement.

**"**

I feel good about everything that happened with the band. I have no complaints or regrets.

**"**

Harry, on 1D's break-up, interview with Paul McCartney, *Another Man*, June 7, 2017.

CHAPTER
**TWO**

# NEW
# DIRECTION

One Direction ruled the pop roost
with a reign that endured five years at the
top of the pops. However, such success
could not be sustained forever, and in
2015 the group initiated an exit strategy,
or "extended hiatus", that broke the
hearts of millions of their fans.

Thankfully, from the ashes of their
demise, a feather-boa'd phoenix would
rise ready to conquer the world all over
again… all on his own. Harry Styles, the
solo artist, was born… but was the pop-
world prepared for his debut album?

**66**

There is very much a respect between all of us. And that is something that you can't really undo. We have a very deep love for each other.

**99**

Harry, on his former 1D bandmates, interview with Zane Lowe, Apple Music, May 17, 2022.

66

It didn't feel scary to me.
The idea of making something
I wasn't 100 per cent behind is
much scarier to me.

99

Harry, about his debut album, interview with
Tony Dokoupil, CBS *Sunday Morning*, October 14, 2017.

---

**"**

I'm enjoying writing at the moment; trying new things. I've been asking myself, 'What do I want to say?'

**"**

Harry, on finding purpose in his music, interview with Paul McCartney, *Another Man*, June 7, 2017.

---

**"**

I didn't want to write stories. I wanted to write my stories, things that happened to me. The number one thing was I wanted to be honest. I hadn't done that before.

**"**

Harry, on his debut album, interview with
Cameron Crowe, *Rolling Stone*, April 18, 2017.

As the face and voice of One Direction – let's be honest – Harry (and the others!) sold more than 80 million albums in their five-year reign at the top of pop.

66

After I'd come out of the band,
I wanted to be taken seriously
as a musician. So, I decided
I can't make fun music.

99

Harry, on the tone of his debut album *Harry Styles*,
interview with Lou Stoppard, *Better Homes and Garden*,
April 26, 2022.

> **"**
> I really wanted to make an album that I wanted to listen to.
> That was the only way I knew I wouldn't look back on it and regret it. It was more, 'What do I want to sit and listen to?' rather than, 'How do I shape up compared to what's on radio right now?'
> **"**

Harry, on his debut album, interview with Joe Coscarelli, *New York Times*, May 11, 2017.

---

**"**

We happen to be in a time where things happening around the world are absolutely impossible to ignore – just the state of the world at the moment. I think it would've been strange to not acknowledge what was going on at all. 'Sign of the Times', for example, is me commenting on how difficult things are.

**"**

Harry, on 'Sign of the Times', interview with Joe Coscarelli, *New York Times*, May 11, 2017.

---

**66**

After the band ended, all I thought about was stressing about what the first album was going to be. *Dunkirk* gave me a chance to completely step away from it for a bit and have a real break.

Harry, on starring in *Dunkirk*, interview with Cameron Crowe, *Rolling Stone*, April 18, 2017.

> **"**
> Being in the band, I always felt we were really young. But I'm not that young anymore. So, how do I play that game of remaining exciting?
> **"**

Harry, on trying to stay relevant with his fans, interview with Zane Lowe, Apple Music, May 17, 2022.

For the first two years
of his career as the biggest
singer in the world, Harry
slept on a mattress in
an attic of his friend Ben
Winston's house in London's
Hampstead Heath.

"No one ever found out,"
Winston recalled to *Rolling
Stone*. "He made our house
a home. And when he moved
out, we were gutted."

> **"**
> I love that album so much
> because it represents such a
> time in my life, but when
> I listen to it – sonically and
> lyrically, especially – I can
> hear places where I was
> playing it safe. I was scared
> to get it wrong.
> **"**

Harry, on his debut album, interview with Shirley Halperin, *Variety*, November 10, 2020.

**"**

I don't think people want to hear me talk about going to bars, and how great everything is. The champagne popping… who wants to hear about it? I don't want to hear my favourite artists talk about all the amazing shit they get to do. I want to hear, 'How did you feel when you were alone in that hotel room, because you chose to be alone?'

**"**

Harry, on the perils of fame, interview with Cameron Crowe, *Rolling Stone*, April 18, 2017.

66

I didn't want to put out my first
album and critics be like, 'He's
tried to recreate the Sixties,
Seventies, Eighties, Nineties.'
Loads of amazing music was
written then, but I'm not saying
I wish I lived back then. I wanted
to do something that sounds
like me.

99

Harry, on his debut album, interview with
Cameron Crowe, *Rolling Stone*, April 18, 2017.

66

When we started, I didn't know what it was going to sound like, or what I wanted it to sound like.

99

Harry, on his debut album, interview with Joe Coscarelli, *New York Times*, May 11, 2017.

> 66
>
> When I started I really didn't know what I was doing. I tried to write as much as possible, with as many different people as possible and try and learn as much as I could. I guarantee I wrote a lot of really, really bad shit before I wrote anything good.
>
> 99

Harry, on the evolution of his songwriting, interview with Timothée Chalamet, *i-D* magazine, December 27, 2019.

"

Sitting at an instrument, you allow yourself to be vulnerable in a different way to speaking to anyone, even if you know them really well.

"

Harry, on his songwriting, interview with Dan Wooton, *The Sun*, May 17, 2017.

**66**

I didn't want to be around distractions. I just wanted to really dive into it and immerse myself. The album became this fluid thing that we were just doing all of the time, rather than going in from 9 to 5. I also didn't want to be around people who might tell me what the music should sound like. So, I went to Jamaica.

**99**

Harry, on writing his debut album in Jamaica, interview with Joe Coscarelli, *New York Times*, May 11, 2017.

> **It's good to have people who can tell you you're an idiot and tell you when you're wrong. I think that's as important as having people geeing you up sometimes.**

Harry, on not taking fame too seriously, interview with Paul McCartney, *Another Man*, June 7, 2017.

66

When they told me we
were doing a movie
on a beach, I had very
different ideas!

99

Harry, on filming *Dunkirk*, interview with
Timothée Chalamet, *i-D* magazine, December 27, 2019.

**"**

# It's easy to have a pop at the kids from *X Factor*.

**"**

Harry, on being an ex-*X Factor* contestant, interview with Jonathan Heaf, *GQ*, August 24, 2015.

**66**

It was time for me to have to make some decisions for myself and not be able to hide behind anyone else. As a person, too. Everything, workwise, that I'd done since I was 16 was made in a democracy.

**99**

Harry, on becoming his own person during the recording of his debut album, interview with Joe Coscarelli, *New York Times*, May 11, 2017.

CHAPTER
**THREE**

# STORY OF MY LIFE

Underneath the façade of his fame,
fortune and fabulousness, Harry Styles
is just a human being like the rest of us,
as the candour and charm of the quotes
uncovered in this chapter conclude.

If you're looking for the real Harry Styles,
the human, stop. You've found him.
He's in here…

**"**

We have a choice, every single day that we wake up, of what we can put into the world, and I ask you to please choose love every single day.

**"**

Harry, speaking at a concert following the Manchester Arena bombing, May 23, 2017.

> **"**
> That was quite a weird time.
> I remember crying about it.
> I didn't really get what was
> going on properly, I was just
> sad that my parents wouldn't
> be together anymore.
> **"**

Harry, on his parents' divorce when he was seven,
interview with Cameron Crowe, *Rolling Stone*,
April 18, 2017.

**"**

I just sang at home, in the shower, in your bedroom, that type of thing. I guess it started again when my friends were in a band and they wanted to do this battle of the bands competition that was at school, and they needed a singer, and one of my friends asked me. We sang 'Are You Gonna Be My Girl' by Jet, and 'Summer of '69'.

**"**

Harry, on his White Eskimo days, interview with Brian Hiatt, *Rolling Stone*, April 11, 2012.

**"**

When I see photos from that day, I think: Relationships are hard, at any age. But at the heart of it I just wanted it to be a normal date.

**"**

Harry, on his first date in New York with Taylor Swift, interview with Cameron Crowe, *Rolling Stone*, April 18, 2017.

**"**

In the last two years, I've become a lot more content with who I am. I think there's so much masculinity in being vulnerable and allowing yourself to be feminine.

**"**

Harry, on masculinity, interview with Timothée Chalamet, *i-D* Magazine, November 2, 2018.

---

66

I didn't grow up in poverty by any means, but we didn't have much money, and I had an expectation of what I could achieve in life. To be where I am, I feel so lucky.

99

Harry, on his immense wealth and success, interview with Lou Stoppard, *Better Homes and Garden*, April 26, 2022.

---

**"**

# I have a private life. You just don't know about it.

**"**

Harry, on keeping his personal life private, interview with Tom Lamont, *The Guardian*, December 14, 2019.

66

I had a really nice upbringing.
I feel very lucky. I had a great
family and always felt loved.
There's nothing worse than an
inauthentic tortured person.

99

Harry, on his childhood, interview with Cameron Crowe,
*Rolling Stone*, April 18, 2017.

**"**

My dad knew I was going to
be famous. I used to listen
to a lot of the music he was
playing. He'd play Elvis Presley
to death, the Stones. I'd sing
along to that and he'd say,
'You're going to be famous.'

**"**

Harry, on becoming famous, interview with Brian Hiatt,
*Rolling Stone*, April 11, 2012.

> **"**
> I had a great childhood.
> I'll admit it. My mom is very
> strong. She has the greatest
> heart. Her house in Cheshire
> is where I go when I want
> to spend some me time.
> **"**

Harry, on his mother Anne Twist, and her home in
Cheshire, interview with Cameron Crowe, *Rolling Stone*,
April 18, 2017.

**"**

I sing in a band with some friends from school. I'm the lead singer. We entered the battle of the bands competition, and we won. Winning that competition and playing in front of lots of people made me realise that that is what I want to do. I got such a thrill when I was singing in front of people it made me want to do more and more.

**"**

Harry, on his first band White Eskimo, *X Factor* audition, April 11, 2010.

66

We wrote a couple of songs,
One was called 'Gone in a
Week'. It was about luggage.
'I'll be gone in a week or
two/Trying to find myself
someplace new/I don't need
any jackets or shoes/The only
luggage I need is you.'

99

Harry, on his first band White Eskimo, interview with
Cameron Crowe, *Rolling Stone*, April 18, 2017.

66

One hundred sixty quid, between all four of us. Forty quid each... We said we'd do it, and then we found out it was the weekend coming up. In three days, we learned 25 songs.

99

Harry, on his first paid gig, a wedding, with White Eskimo, interview with Brian Hiatt, *Rolling Stone*, April 11, 2012.

66

I lived with both parents, and then moved with my mum, and we owned a pub for five years. I remember the first night, a band was playing downstairs, and I just thought, 'How am I going to get to sleep with this noise?' By the end, I could fall asleep next to the band, I was so used to the noise.

99

Harry, on living above a pub in his childhood, interview with Brian Hiatt, *Rolling Stone*, April 11, 2012.

# £6

Harry's hourly wage at
the W Mandeville bakery
in Holmes Chapel, his
first job.*

*Today, Harry earns an estimated $2.25 million
*every single night* he performs a concert,
according to *Billboard*.

66

# I don't get a nice bun on my break anymore.

99

Harry, on the perks of working in a bakery versus being a popstar, interview with Brian Hiatt, *Rolling Stone*, April 11, 2012.

> "
> I could always hear my sister's music at the top of the stairs and I used to pretend to have a guitar and perform in my mirror in my bedroom.
> "

Harry, on his first performances, *One Direction: This Is Us*, 2013.

> **66**
>
> I watched *Pulp Fiction* when I was probably too young. But when I was 13, I saved up money from my paper route to buy a 'Bad Motherfucker' wallet. Just a stupid white kid in the English countryside with that wallet.
>
> **99**

Harry, on his favourite movie, interview with Rob Sheffield, *Rolling Stone*, August 26, 2019.

CHAPTER
**FOUR**

# GOLDEN BOY

With the arrival of Harry Styles, the serious solo artist, stamped into stone with his debut album in 2017, Harry would go on to capitalize on his songwriting success with his 2020 sophomore record, arena tour, and a period of his life that Harry would use to re-evaluate and rediscover who he was all over again.

The quotes in this chapter shine a light on the artist's ever-evolving dedication to his craft and his own mental health during his fantastic *Fine Line* period.

**"**

I just don't think you need to be a dick to be a good artist. But then, there are also a lot of good artists who are dicks. So, hmm. Maybe I need to start scaring babies in supermarkets?

**"**

Harry, on his nice guy reputation, interview with Tom Lamont, *The Guardian*, December 14, 2019.

**"**

# He'd be very confused. He would be very confused!

**"**

Harry, when asked what his 16-year-old self would think of how far he'd come, interview with Tony Dokoupil, CBS *Sunday Morning*, October 14, 2017.

66

There's so much joy to be had in playing with clothes. I've never really thought too much about what it means — it just becomes this extended part of creating something.

99

Harry, on his fashion style, *Vogue*, December 2020.

---

66

When you're making music,
it feels really creative. A large
part of acting is doing nothing,
waiting. I don't find that section
of it to be that fulfilling. I like
doing it in the moment, but
I don't think I'll do it a lot.

99

Harry, on acting, interview with Brittany Spanos,
*Rolling Stone*, August 22, 2022.

---

**"**

I just want to make stuff that is right,
that is fun, in terms of the process,
that I can be proud of for a long time,
that my friends can be proud of,
that my family can be proud of, that
my kids will be proud of one day.

**"**

Harry, on feeling proud of his art, interview with
Lou Stoppard, *Better Homes and Garden*, April 26, 2022.

---

**"**

# When do I feel my most beautiful? Maybe when I'm asleep.

**"**

Harry, when asked when he feels his most beautiful,
interview with Lynette Nylander, *Dazed and Confused*,
November 15, 2021.

---

**"**

In music, I am somewhat in my comfort zone. But in movies, when I show up, I'm the new guy.

**"**

Harry, on acting, interview with Lynette Nylander, *Dazed and Confused*, November 15, 2021.

Since going solo
in 2015, Harry has sold
more than 15 million
albums across the three
studio records:

*Harry Styles* (2017),
*Fine Line* (2019)
and
*Harry's House* (2022).

66

To not wear something because it's females' clothing, you shut out a whole world of great clothes. And I think what's exciting about right now is you can wear what you like. It doesn't have to be X or Y. Those lines are becoming more and more blurred.

99

Harry, on his fashion choices and stage outfits, interview with Shirley Halperin, *Variety*, November 10, 2020.

**66**

By the time we went out touring the *Fine Line* album, I'd finished *Harry's House*. I got to play those songs from *Fine Line* with the knowledge of what was next. I feel like I got to hide a secret this whole time.

**99**

Harry, on writing two albums back to back, interview with Zane Lowe, Apple Music, May 17, 2022.

**"**

It's always nice to know that people like what you're doing, but ultimately I don't put too much weight on it. It's important when making any kind of art to remove the ego from it.

**"**

Harry, on his music, interview with Shirley Halperin, *Variety*, November 10, 2020.

**"**

With the second album I let go of
the fear of getting it wrong and… it
was really joyous and really free.
I think with music it's so important to
evolve – and that extends to clothes
and videos. That's why you look back
at David Bowie with Ziggy Stardust or
the Beatles and their different eras –
that fearlessness is super inspiring.

**"**

Harry, on fear as inspiration, interview with
Hamish Bowles, *Vogue*, November 13, 2020.

66

As a kid I definitely liked fancy dress. In a school play, I was cast as Barney, a church mouse. I remember it was crazy to me that I was wearing a pair of tights. But that was maybe where it all kicked off!

99

Harry, on his love of fancy dress, interview with Hamish Bowles, *Vogue*, November 13, 2020.

> ❝
> Am I sprinkling in nuggets of sexual ambiguity to try and be more interesting? No.
> ❞

Harry, on his clothing choices, interview with Tom Lamont, *The Guardian*, December 14, 2019.

**"**

When you meet people who
are successful and aren't nice,
you think: What's your excuse?
Because I've met the other sort.

**"**

Harry, on staying humble, interview with Tom Lamont,
*The Guardian*, December 14, 2019.

66

Making *Fine Line*, the times where I was really happy were the happiest of my life, but the times where I was a little lower were the saddest times.

99

Harry, on *Fine Line*, interview with Ben Homewood, *Music Week Interview*, December 9, 2019.

> **"**
> My first album wasn't necessarily
> a radio record, but I could tour it
> and people came to the shows and
> enjoyed them, and it made me feel
> I had some sort of freedom to make
> what I wanted to, and I wanted
> to make some fun songs again.
> **"**

Harry, on his first two albums, interview with
Ben Homewood, *Music Week Interview*,
December 9, 2019.

> 66
>
> I'd seen this clip of David Bowie talking about how you usually end up doing your best work when you feel like you can't quite touch the bottom, and I realised that I like doing things that made me feel uncomfortable.
>
> 99

Harry, on jumping out of your comfort zone, interview with Ben Homewood, *Music Week Interview*, December 9, 2019.

**"**

I write from my experiences; everyone does that. That's what hits your heart. That's the stuff that's hardest to say, and it's the stuff I talk least about.

Harry, on writing songs from experience, interview with Cameron Crowe, *Rolling Stone*, April 18, 2017.

66

With an artist like Prince all you wanted to do was know more. And that mystery – it's why those people are so magical! Like, I don't know what Prince eats for breakfast. That mystery… it's just what I like.

99

Harry, on artists who keep a sense of mystery, interview with Cameron Crowe, *Rolling Stone*, April 18, 2017.

**"**

I'm really enjoying making music and experimenting way too much to see myself doing a full switch, to go back and do that again. Because I also think if we went back to doing things the same way, it wouldn't be the same, anyway.

**"**

Harry, on a possible 1D future reunion, interview with Rob Sheffield, *Rolling Stone*, August 26, 2019.

66

I've never done an interview and said,
'So I was in a relationship, and this
is what happened.' Because, for me,
music is where I let that cross over.
It's the only place, strangely, where it
feels right to let music do the talking.

99

Harry, on letting his music do the talking about previous
relationships, interview with Rob Sheffield, *Rolling Stone*,
August 26, 2019.

66

In the moment where you really let yourself be in that zone of being vulnerable, you reach this feeling of openness. That's when you feel like, 'Oh, I'm fucking living, man.'

99

Harry, on meditation and therapy, interview with Rob Sheffield, *Rolling Stone*, August 26, 2019.

66

I get them a lot when I'm driving.
I'll be listening to something, and
I'll go back to when I was 12 and
I'll think, 'Shit, if my 12-year-old self
could see me now'. I think it's really
important to have those moments.

99

Harry, on moments of reflection, interview with
Timothée Chalamet, *i-D* magazine, December 27, 2019.

CHAPTER
**FIVE**

# AS IT WAS

With the release of *Harry's House* in 2022, and his pursuing Love On Tour 2022–2023 globe-trotting circus, the real Harry Styles was unveiled to his fans. Funny, frank, forthright and fabulously fashionable, this Harry Styles went beyond all expectations, and with 'As It Was' – the biggest worldwide hit of 2022 – he became the most Googled, ogled and YouTubed performer of the 21st century.

We all live in Harry's house now. Come on in, and take a sneak-peek inside his drawers…

> "
>
> After everything that's happened over the last two and half, three years, I think the sentiment of – it's not the same as it was – felt pretty perfect.
>
> "

Harry, about 'As It Was' being the first single from *Harry's House* and COVID, interview with Bru Baker, *Audacy*, April 1, 2022.

66

In music, there's such an immediate response to what you do. You finish a song and people clap. When you're filming a movie and they say 'Cut,' you expect everyone to start clapping, but they don't. Everyone just goes back to doing their jobs, and you're like, 'Oh, shit, was it that bad?'

99

Harry, on acting in *Don't Worry Darling*, interview with Brittany Spanos, *Rolling Stone*, August 22, 2022.

"

We came offstage, and I went into my dressing room and just wanted to sit by myself for a minute. After One Direction, I didn't expect to ever experience anything new. I felt like, 'All right, I've seen how crazy it can get.' And I think there was something about it where I was ... not terrified, but I just needed a minute. Because I wasn't sure what it was. Just that the energy felt *insane*.

"

Harry, on performing "As It Was" for first time after it became No.1 worldwide, interview with Brittany Spanos, *Rolling Stone*, August 22, 2022.

66

It's really unnatural to stand in front of that many people and take a shower. You're just a naked person, in your most vulnerable, human form. Just like a naked baby, basically.

99

Harry, on his post-show backstage ritual of immediately showering after a show, interview with Julianna Piskorz, *Evening Standard*, August 23, 2022.

> 66
>
> We didn't really know what we were going in for. It just felt like sitting at home doing nothing might feel better if we all move in together and try to make some music.
>
> 99

Harry, on moving in with his songwriters to write *Harry's House*, interview with Brittany Spanos, *Rolling Stone*, August 22, 2022.

66

Finally, I won't feel like my life is over if *Harry's House* isn't a commercial success.

99

Harry, on having nothing left to prove, interview with Lou Stoppard, *Better Homes and Garden*, April 26, 2022.

'As It Was' is the most-streamed track worldwide on Spotify in 24 hours by a male artist. It was listened to more than 16 million times in its first day – a Guinness World Record.

In one year it amassed 1.5 billion plays and spent ten weeks at No.1 on the UK charts and 15 weeks as No.1 on the *Billboard* Top 100 in the U.S.

66

I don't think of myself
as a style icon... bringing
people together at my
shows is the thing I'm
most proud of.

99

Harry, on performing live, interview with Lynette Nylander,
*Dazed and Confused*, November 15, 2021.

"

Putting out the first single ['As It Was'] from *Harry's House* was far and away the most relaxed I've ever felt putting anything out. I no longer feel like my overall happiness is dependent on whether a song does well.

"

Harry, on 'As It Was', interview with Zane Lowe, Apple Music, May 17, 2022.

66

I was in a sushi restaurant in Los Angeles when one of my songs came on from the last album [*Fine Line*]. It was really strange music for a sushi restaurant! And then I was like – that would be a really fun album title.

99

Harry, on the song 'Music for a Sushi Restaurant'*, interview with Leila Fadel, NPR, May 20, 2022.

*"It'll be everything I've ever wanted," Harry said, if he ever hears 'Music for a Sushi Restaurant' in a sushi restaurant.

"

I get a front-row seat to see a bunch of people getting in a room together and just being themselves, dancing like nobody's watching. A room full of people just loving each other is so powerful.

Harry, on the power of live music, interview with Lynette Nylander, *Dazed and Confused*, November 15, 2021.

66

The crowd is so emotionally generous that they just want me to be having a good time, and I can feel that. Doing shows is my favourite thing to do in the world.

99

Harry, on performing live, interview with Zane Lowe, Apple Music, May 17, 2022.

66

'As It Was' is definitely the highest volume of men that I would get stopping me to say something about it. That feels like a weird comment because it's not like men was the goal. It's just something I noticed.

99

Harry, on 'As It Was', interview with Brittany Spanos, *Rolling Stone*, August 22, 2022.

> **"**
> I realized that that home
> feeling isn't something that
> you get from a house; it's
> more of an internal thing.
> You realize that when
> you stop for a minute.
> **"**

Harry, on home and the title of *Harry's House*, interview
with Lou Stoppard, *Better Homes and Garden*,
April 26, 2022.

**"**

I don't think being beautiful
or feeling beautiful is about
looking good. When people
are happy and glowing,
they're radiating beauty.

**"**

Harry, on defining beauty, interview with Lynette Nylander,
*Dazed and Confused*, November 15, 2021.

66

# It sounds like the biggest, and the most fun album, but it's by far the most intimate.

99

Harry, on *Harry's House*, interview with Lou Stoppard, *Better Homes and Garden*, April 26, 2022.

66

For a really long time, I was terrified
of what my life was if I wasn't making
music. During lockdown, I stopped
for a second and thought, 'What does
it actually mean to make something?
And what does it mean to me to
make something as my job?'

99

Harry, on the art of making, interview with Zane Lowe,
Apple Music, May 17, 2022.

---

**66**

# I have unlocked an ability to be myself completely, unapologetically.

**99**

Harry, on Harry, interview with Lynette Nylander, *Dazed and Confused*, November 15, 2021.

---

> ❝
>
> It was very kind of literal and on the nose: I wanted to make an acoustic EP and make it all in my house and make it really intimate. I named it *Harry's House* after Haruomi Horsono, who had an album in the '70s called *Horsono House.*
>
> ❞

Harry, on the title of *Harry's House*, interview with Zane Lowe, Apple Music, May 17, 2022.

**"**

When it comes to relationships, you just expect yourself to be good at it… but being in a real relationship with someone is a skill.

**"**

Harry, on dating, interview with Hamish Bowles, *Vogue*, November 13, 2020.

> "
> You can never be overdressed. There's no such thing. The people that I looked up to in music – Prince and David Bowie and Elvis and Freddie Mercury and Elton John – they're such showmen. As a kid it was completely mind-blowing.
> "

Harry, on his influences as inspiration, interview with Hamish Bowles, *Vogue*, November 13, 2020.

66
The coolest things are not
always the cool things.
Do you know what I mean?
99

Harry, on cool things, interview with Tom Lamont,
*The Guardian*, December 14, 2019.

"

What I like about acting is I feel like I have no idea what I'm doing. It's fun to play in worlds that aren't necessary your own.

"

Harry, on acting in *Don't Worry Darling* (2022), interview with Manori Ravindran, *Variety*, September 5, 2022.

> **66**
> I wanted the song to be
> a mantra for the tour. It's
> universal and important, a
> small change that makes a
> big difference. It's just, 'Treat
> people with kindness...'
> **99**

Harry, on creating a tour fuelled by kindness, interview
with Ben Homewood, *Music Week Interview*,
December 9, 2019.

"

People ask for advice and I by no means feel like I'm in a place to give it because I feel like I still don't know anything. Ultimately the only thing I try to remember is that music is so subjective.

"

Harry, on giving advice to young musicians, interview with Ben Homewood, *Music Week Interview*, December 9, 2019.

---

**66**

I had a wonderful experience
being directed by Olivia. Acting is
kind of very uncomfortable at times.
I think you have to trust a lot. It
requires a lot of trust if you want to
kind of give it everything, and I think
being able to trust your director is
a gift, so that was very helpful.

**99**

Harry, on being directed by his then-girlfriend
Olivia Wilde for *Don't Worry Darling*, interview with
Howard Stern, SiriusFM, March 4, 2020.

---

**"**

You know my favourite thing about the movie? Like it feels like a movie. It feels like a real go-to-the-theatre film movie that you know is kind of the reason why you go to watch something on the big screen.

**"**

Harry, on *Don't Worry Darling* being an entertaining film, in a PR clip that went viral, PR junket, September 5, 2022.

**❝**

Yes, I was robbed on Valentine's Day – that's what you get for being single these days! I should have had other plans.

**❞**

Harry, on being robbed of his phone and money in New York, interview with Howard Stern, SiriusFM, March 4, 2020.

66

Just because you're in a band with someone doesn't mean you have to be best friends. That's not always how it works. I think even in the disagreements, there's always a mutual respect for each other.

99

Harry, on his relationship with other 1D members, interview with Rob Sheffield, *Rolling Stone*, August 26, 2019.

66

I don't want a lot of credit for being a feminist. I grew up with my mum and my sister – when you grow up around women, your female influence is just bigger. Of course men and women should be equal. That doesn't feel like a crazy thing to me. I think the ideals of feminism are pretty straightforward.

99

Harry, on feminism, interview with Rob Sheffield, *Rolling Stone*, August 26, 2019.

> **"**
> We'd do mushrooms, lie down on the grass, and listen to Paul McCartney's *Ram* in the sunshine.
> **"**

Harry, on recording *Harry's House* and *Fine Line*, interview with Rob Sheffield, *Rolling Stone*, August 26, 2019.

**"**

I want to make people feel comfortable being whatever they want to be. Maybe at a show you can have a moment of knowing that you're not alone.

**"**

Harry, about his first world tour and performing live, interview with Rob Sheffield, *Rolling Stone*, August 26, 2019.

> **"**
> I was a little nervous to champion a cause because the last thing I wanted was for it to feel like I was saying, 'Look at me! I'm the good guy!'
> **"**

Harry, on being a LBTQ+ icon, interview with
Rob Sheffield, *Rolling Stone*, August 26, 2019.

66

When I was in the band, I always
knew what I was doing two years in
advance. Now, I'm making records
on my own it's pretty exciting
because I know this is all I'm going
to be doing until I finish the record.
It's a new way of working.

99

Harry, on working to his own schedule, interview with
Timothée Chalamet, *i-D* magazine, December 27, 2019.

66

Everything in my life has felt like a bonus since *The X Factor.*

99

Harry, on life post 1D, interview with Brittany Spanos, *Rolling Stone*, August 22, 2022.

> 66
>
> I exercise every day and take care of my body, so why wouldn't I do that with my mind? So many of your emotions are so foreign before you start analyzing them properly.
>
> 99

Harry, on therapy, interview with Brittany Spanos, *Rolling Stone*, August 22, 2022.

> **"**
> I'll put on something that feels really flamboyant, and I don't feel crazy wearing it. I think if you get something that you feel amazing in, it's like a superhero outfit.
> **"**

Harry, on his clothing styles, interview with Hamish Bowles, *Vogue*, November 13, 2020.

66

There's hundreds and thousands,
if not millions, of musicians who are
so far superior to me. I do believe
some people make their own luck,
but I also think so much of it is about
luck and timing. When I look at it,
there's no reason for it to have been
me who got to do this for a living.

99

Harry, on becoming a famous musician, interview with
Howard Stern, SiriusFM, March 4, 2020.

66

While I was in the band, I was constantly scared I might sing a wrong note. I felt so much weight in terms of not getting things wrong. Now, as a solo artist, I feel like the fans have given me an environment to be myself and grow up and create this safe space to learn and make mistakes.

99

Harry, on being in 1D, interview with Rob Sheffield, *Rolling Stone*, August 26, 2019.

66

When I'm working, I work really hard, and I think I'm really professional. Then when I'm not, I'm not. I'd like to think I'm open, and probably quite stubborn, too, and willing to be vulnerable. I can be selfish sometimes, but I'd like to think that I'm a caring person.

99

Harry, on Harry, interview with Brittany Spanos, *Rolling Stone*, August 22, 2022.

> **"**
> Sometimes people say,
> 'You've only publicly been with
> women,' and I don't think I've
> publicly been with anyone.
> If someone takes a picture of
> you with someone, it doesn't
> mean you're choosing to
> have a public relationship.
> **"**

Harry, on his private life made public, interview with
Brittany Spanos, *Rolling Stone*, August 22, 2022

66

The fantasy or the version of you that people can build you up to be feels like a person that isn't flawed. What I value the most from my friends is I'm constantly reminded that it's OK to be flawed. I think I'm pretty messy and make mistakes.

99

Harry, on being flawed despite what fans think, interview with Brittany Spanos, *Rolling Stone*, August 22, 2022.

> 66
>
> It was the last song that was written for the album. It was written in the countryside in England, and it's one of my favourite songs on the album. It's about embracing change, losing oneself, finding oneself. 99

Harry, about 'As It Was', interview with Greg James, BBC Radio 1, April 1, 2022.

---

**66**

# I think I was just a show-off. I say that like it's past tense.

**99**

Harry, on singing since he was four years old, interview with Brittany Spanos, *Rolling Stone*, August 22, 2022.

---

# CHAPTER
## SIX

# CHERRY ON TOP

For the past decade, and more,
Harry has given the world more than
just incredible music and a beautiful life
philosophy. He's a quote machine too,
giving journalists and interviewers a
litany of killer soundbites and one-liners
too good to not include here as
a greatest hits package.

So sit back, relax, and let Harry's
dulcet tones calm your nerves one last
time, with this compilation of
his most cheeky wit and wisdom…

**"**

Some of them are funny. Some of them are ridiculous. Some of them are annoying. I don't want to be one of those people that complains about the rumours.

**"**

Harry, on the constant rumours concerning his love life, *GQ*, September 2013.

66

If you make your life about the fact that you can't go anywhere and everything has to be a big deal, then that's what your life becomes. Now, in London, I walk everywhere.

99

Harry, on the theatre of fame, interview with Brittany Spanos, *Rolling Stone*, August 22, 2022.

Harry's 2022–2023 Love On Tour world jaunt played to 5 million people, across 173 shows, including a record-breaking 18-night residency at California's Kia Forum, 20 nights at New York's Madison Square Garden, and broke attendance records at his Wembley Stadium, London, concerts. Harry described the tour as "the greatest experience of my life". The tour also raised $6.5 million for charity.

> **"**
> The most loving thing you can do is see someone's imperfections, and not love them in spite of that, but love them because of that.
> **"**

Harry, on love and relationships, interview with Brittany Spanos, *Rolling Stone*, August 22, 2022.

> ❝
> My producer keeps asking
> me when I'm going to have
> my big breakdown.
> ❞

Harry, on mega-fame becoming too much to handle,
interview with Lou Stoppard, *Better Homes and Garden*,
April 26, 2022.

66

I think that accepting living, being happy, hurting in the extremes, that is the most alive you can be. Losing it crying, losing it laughing – there's no way to feel more alive than that.

99

Harry, on feeling alive, interview with Lou Stoppard, *Better Homes and Garden*, April 26, 2022.

66

Working out who I could trust was stressful. At the time, there were still the kiss-and-tells. But I think I got to a place where I was like, why do I feel ashamed? I'm a 26-year-old man who's single; it's like, yes, I have sex.

99

Harry, on the end of 1D, trust and his sex life, interview with Lou Stoppard, *Better Homes and Garden*, April 26, 2022.

66

I think if you're making what you want to make, then ultimately no one can tell you you're unsuccessful, because you're doing what makes you happy.

99

Harry, on happiness, interview with Mary Louise Kelly, NPR, February 27, 2020.

**"**

I've been trying to read and educate myself so that in 20 years I'm still doing the right things and taking the right steps. I believe in karma, and I think it's just a time right now where we could use a little more kindness and empathy and patience with people, be a little more prepared to listen and grow.

**"**

Harry, on his mantra of "treating people with kindness", interview with Hamish Bowles, *Vogue*, November 13, 2020.

---

**"**

I sometimes feel like I'm supposed to be floating on this cloud of success and happiness, and obviously that's not how it works. I think through my own sense of self and personal journey, I am realising that happiness isn't this kind of end state.

**"**

Harry, on happiness, interview with Lynette Nylander, *Dazed and Confused*, November 15, 2021.

---

> **"**
> I love the feeling of
> nobody knowing where
> I am, that kind of
> escape… and freedom.
> **"**

Harry, on feeling free, interview with Hamish Bowles, *Vogue*, November 13, 2020.

> **"**
> The moment you feel more comfortable with yourself, everything becomes a lot easier.
> **"**

Harry, on Harry, interview with Tom Lamont,
*The Guardian*, December 14, 2019.

> **"**
> I watched a film at my house with a girl. I don't remember what we watched though!
> **"**

Harry, on his first date, interview with Ella Lawrence, *Seventeen* magazine, March 9, 2012.

> 66
>
> In terms of how I want to dress,
> I tend to make decisions with
> collaborators I want to work with.
> I want things to look a certain way.
> Not because it makes me look
> gay, or it makes me look straight,
> or it makes me look bisexual, but
> because I think it looks cool.
>
> 99

Harry, on being cool, interview with Tom Lamont,
*The Guardian*, December 14, 2019.

66

I wouldn't say I'm girl crazy, because that makes me sound like a bit of a womaniser. That isn't really me.

99

Harry, on suddenly having screaming fans, *Seventeen* magazine, November 2012.

66

I like having fun but it's nice to just wake up in your own bed, isn't it? I think I've got my head screwed on. I do have a lot of fun but I'm not half as busy as I'm made out to be, that's for sure. I'm doing stuff that every other 18-year-old lad is doing but it gets written about.

99

Harry, on having "fun", *Seventeen* magazine, November 2012.

**"**

One of the reasons why I don't like the word 'famous' is because then people use it afterwards. They go, like: 'He used to be famous but he is not famous anymore.' I was a guy before fame, I was the same guy during and I'm the same guy afterwards, but people think they can label your life.

**"**

Harry, on being famous, *One Direction: This Is Us*, August 2013.

66

I used to say the age limit was any woman older than my mum – who is 43 – but...

99

Harry, on his penchant for dating older women, interview with Tom Bryant, *Daily Mirror*, November 12, 2012.

**"**

## According to the papers, I have, like, 7,000 girlfriends.

**"**

Harry, on press speculation about his dating life, interview with Tom Bryant, *Daily Mirror*, November 12, 2012.

**"**

It's really hard to go from doing a show with thousands of people there to your hotel room – from being around people to nothing. After five years of doing that, I learnt a lot about myself.

**"**

Harry, on isolation and loneliness, interview with Dan Wooton, *The Sun*, May 17, 2017.

66

Stripping off is very liberating. I feel so free. I think you could safely say I'm not shy.

99

Harry, on being naked, interview with Dan Wooton, *The Sun*, May 17, 2017.

66

I want to shave my hair off,
and no one will really let me.
Everyone's telling me not to
do it. And my argument is,
like, I think my popularity is
in my face, and not my hair.

99

Harry, on his then-famously long hair, interview with
Nick Grimshaw, BBC Radio One, February 21, 2013.

66

When somebody gets out of a band, they go, 'That wasn't me. I was held back.' But it was me. I don't feel like I was held back at all. It was so much fun. If I didn't enjoy it, I wouldn't have done it. It's not like I was tied to a radiator.

99

Harry, on 1D breaking up, interview with Rob Sheffield, *Rolling Stone*, August 26, 2019.

66

Teenage girls have a bullshit detector. You want honest people as your audience. We're so past that dumb outdated narrative of 'Oh, these people are girls, so they don't know what they're talking about.' They're the ones who know what they're talking about! They're the people who listen obsessively. They fucking own this shit. They're running it.

99

Harry, on his teenage girl fans, interview with Rob Sheffield, *Rolling Stone*, August 26, 2019.

> **❝**
>
> To everyone who came out to see us play, thank you. You have given me memories that will last a lifetime, more than I could have ever dreamed of. Thank you for your time, your energy, and your love. Look after each other, I'll see you again when the time is right. Treat People With Kindness. I love you more than you'll ever know.
>
> **❞**

Harry, his final words to fans on his last Love On Tour date, RCF Arena, Reggio Emilia, Italy, July 22, 2023.

**"**

When people say you're 'famous', it gives you no substance. It's not like saying, 'He was a really nice guy' or 'He was really funny'. It's just like weird. I hate it.

**"**

Harry, on fame, *One Direction: This Is Us*, 2013.

66

If you can step outside of the craziness and appreciate it for the fact that it's extraordinary, see it as this amazing thing for a second, fame's alright. If you just think that's how life is, that's when you lose touch.

99

Harry, on not taking fame too seriously, interview with Paul McCartney, *Another Man*, June 7, 2017.

The child's voice at the beginning of 'As It Was' is Harry's goddaughter, Ruby Winston. She calls Harry before bed every night, but one night he missed the call so she left him the song's intro as a voicemail.

"I dug it out one day when I was in the studio, put it at the start of the song," Harry told BBC Radio 2's Zoe Ball in 2022. "And I loved it so it stuck and I hope when she's older she will enjoy looking back on it."

**"**

I feel a noticeable change in how happy I am when I'm not on social media. Someone once described it to me like a house party, where there are three people who are great and 23 people who aren't that nice. You just wouldn't go to that party, would you?

**"**

Harry, on social media, interview with Timothée Chalamet, *i-D* magazine, December 27, 2019.

66

It never gets any easier. The fear just turns into adrenaline. The first few shows you're scared as that's when all the mistakes happen. And then once you get your bearings and you know what you're doing you can enjoy it more. Every show is different so you can't entirely relax, and sometimes I do wonder what I'll be having for tea that night... but I try to remain focused!

99

Harry, on performing every night on tour, interview with Jonathan Heaf, *GQ*, August 24, 2015.

> **"**
> Bisexual? Me? I don't
> think so. I'm pretty
> sure I'm not.
> **"**

Harry, on his sexuality, interview with Jonathan Heaf,
GQ, August 24, 2015.

66

If you give yourself entirely
to the business, you'd end
up going mad. And I'm not
mad. Not yet.

99

Harry, on the music industry, interview with
Jonathan Heaf, *GQ*, August 24, 2015.

---

**"**

I know the number of people I've slept with, yes. It's definitely less than 100...

**"**

Harry, on his love life, interview with Jonathan Heaf, *GQ*, August 24, 2015.

---

66

I don't think you can ever get used to being this famous.

99

Harry, on fame, interview with Jonathan Heaf, *GQ*, August 24, 2015.

> **"**
> I think on nights like tonight it's important for us to remember there is no such thing as 'best' in music. I don't think any of us sit in the studio making decisions on what is going to get us one of these. This doesn't happen to people like me very often and this is so, so nice.
> **"**

Harry, his now-iconic Grammy Award win for *Harry's House*, February 6, 2023.